Autoimmune Paleo Cookbook 2018

The Complete Paleo Autoimmune Protocol Diet Guide- 14 Days Meal Plan to Manage Chronic and Inflammation Diseases

By Mollie Brady

Copyright © 2018 by Mollie Brady

All rights are reserved. All of the rights are reserved by the publisher. Printing, reproducing, transmitting, or copying any part of this book whether in printed, electronic or any format, is not legal without a permission granted by the publisher.

Warning Disclaimer

While we try to keep the information in this cookbook correct and up-to-date, it's for general educational purposes only. There are no warranties or representations, implied or expressed, about the reliability, accuracy, or completeness with respect to the information contained in this cookbook for any purpose. The information is not intended to replace personalized medical diagnosis, counseling and treatment from a health professional. The reader should consult a medical professional in matters concerning their health, particularly to any symptoms that may require medical attention or diagnosis.

The author, editor and publisher shall not be liable for any damages arising here from.

United States of America.

First printing, 2018

ISBN: 9781719987059

Table of Content

Chapter 1 Introduction to the Paleo AIP Diet 1

What are Autoimmune Diseases? 1

The Autoimmune Protocol (AIP) and How It Works 2

What is Autoimmune Protocol (AIP) Diet? 2

What Can I or Cannot Take When on AIP Diet? 3

Common Mistakes to Avoid on AIP Diet 4

AIP Diet versus the Paleo Piet 6

Chapter 2 60 Amazing AIP Diet Recipes 7

AIP Breakfast Recipes 8

Apple-sage Pork Skillet 8

Fries with Bacon Chive Crumble 10

Moroccan Inspired Skillet 12

Porridge with Lemon and Berries 14

Turkey Sausage 16

Risotto with Greens 17

Maple Sage Patties 19

Squash Browns 20

Italian Spiced 50/50 Sausages 21

Plantain Wrap 22

Banana Bread 23

Sticky Buns 25

AIP Lunch Recipes 27

Calamari Summer Salad 28

Shrimp Salad with Cilantro-Lemon Ranch Dressing 30

Carrot, Cucumber, and Avocado Salad 31

Deli-Style Italian Pasta Salad 33

Chicken Vegetable Salad 35

Orange-Glazed Pork Tenderloin 37

Grilled Chicken Thighs with Pineapple Mint Salsa 39

Zuppa Toscana 41

Honey-Lemon Glazed Salmon 42

Wild Salmon with Zucchini Noodles 44

Crispy Drill Fried Fish 46

Avocado Green Smoothie 48

Stuffed Chicken Breast 49

AIP Dinner Recipes 51

Shrimp Scampi 51

Pumpkin Chili 53

Creamy Garlic Spaghetti Squash Casserole 55

Mini Lasagna 57

Chicken Salsa Verde Tacos 59

Italian Calzone 61

Hearty Salmon Chowder 63

Ginger Lemon Sticky Chicken 65

Creamy Leek and Salmon Soup 67

Onion Soup 69

Pomegranate Chicken Salad 71

Baked Chicken Thighs 72

Beef Lettuce Wraps 73

Steak Salad with Arugula 74

Broccoli Beef 75

AIP Snacks and Desserts Recipes 76

Zucchini Fries 76

Tigernut Cheese Cracker 78

Asian Stuffed Mushrooms 80

Salmon Cakes 82

Pumpkin Granola 83

Maple-Cinnamon Sweet Potatoes 84

Raw Strawberry Papaya Ice Cream Tart 85

2-Ingredients Banana Fudge 86

Coconut Plantain Macaroons 88

Chewy Cinnamon Sugar Cookies 89

AIP Drinks Recipes 91

Stone Fruit Smoothie 91

AIP Margarita Mocktail 92

Strawberry-Hibiscus Iced Tea 93

Watermelon-Basil Shrub 94

Strawberry Ginger swizzle 95

AIP Coffee 96

Berry Fizz Mocktail 97

Paleo Cardio Green Juice 98

Pineapple Smoothie 99

Watermelon Aqua Fresca 100

Chapter 3 A 14-day meal plan 101

Chapter 1

Introduction to the Paleo AIP Diet

Hello there!

With this cookbook I hope to bring to you 60 amazing Autoimmune Protocol recipes but first let's take a little detour and explain some of the basic stuff and answer some of the questions you might have brewing up.

What are Autoimmune Diseases?

Now let's talk a little science, autoimmune diseases result from a dysfunction of the immune system. The immune system is meant to shield you from diseases and infections. Though, sometimes the immune system is capable of producing antibodies that end up attacking healthy cells, tissues and organs, this dysfunction leads to autoimmune disease. It can affect basically any part of the body and currently more than 90 variants have been identified, some are widely popular, such as the type1 diabetes, multiple sclerosis, lupus, rheumatoid arthritis and so on while some are rare, hence they are more difficult to diagnose. Even the doctors don't know what cause autoimmune disease just that there are some risk factors that increases the chances of suffering from them like, genetics and environment.

The Autoimmune Protocol (AIP) and How It Works

The autoimmune protocol is a food elimination and food reintroduction process which has been purposely designed for people suffering from autoimmune diseases. The goal is to identify the foods and or ingredients causing the abnormality in the functionality of the immune system. The AIP is meant for turning around of nutrient deficiencies and restore gut micro biome to obtain and re-establish overall health and wellness of both the body and the mind.

In the elimination stage, you remove all foods that can cause autoimmune diseases (like processed food, grains, legumes, dairy; full list comes later) for a particular period of time. This removal will provide opportunity for your gut to heal and improve your immune system. Then slowly reintroduce those foods previously eliminated and see the ones that aggravate or cause the symptoms, thereby developing an eating and living routine that best suits your body and your life style. For full and comprehensive guide on the AIP, a professional nutrition therapist should be consulted.

What is Autoimmune Protocol (AIP) Diet?

Sometimes referred to as paleo autoimmune protocol, the AIP is a system designed in a bid to help reduce inflammation in the body to relieve symptoms of autoimmune disorders. But the questions are: (1) What exactly can you eat on this diet? (2) What benefits can the AIP diet provide? I'll get to answering them right away.

1) What exactly can you eat on this diet? The whole point of the AIP diet is to avoid inflammatory food and go for the nutrient-rich food. This raises another question of which type of food falls into which category? more on that later but for now let us answer the second question
2) What benefits can the AIP diet provide?
- AIP diet helps resets/refresh the Immune System
- It prevents the autoimmune response of the immune system
- It reduces symptoms of autoimmune diseases
- It prevents the occurrence of secondary autoimmune diseases

What Can I or Cannot Take When on AIP Diet?

To-takes: Basically anything not factory made, which still leaves a whole of options which include:

- Meat and fish
- Vegetables (no nightshades like tomatoes, eggplants, peppers and potatoes)
- Sweet potatoes
- Fruit (small quantity)
- Coconut milk
- Avocado, olive and coconut oil
- Honey (usage is occasional and in small quantity)

- Fresh non-seed herbs; basil or oregano will do fine

Don't takes:

- All grains; such as oats, rice and wheat
- All dairy products
- Eggs
- Legumes, such as beans and peanuts
- Nightshade vegetables (tomatoes, peppers, eggplants, potatoes)
- All sugars including all sugar replacements (only exception is the occasional usage of honey)
- Alcohol
- All oils (except for avocado, coconuts and olive)
- Butter

Common Mistakes to Avoid on AIP Diet

Yes, AIP's awesome but people often don't see its significance because of the few simple mistakes they make, I will be trying to highlight some of them here.

- Not taking enough care of physical and mental wellness- yes, the task of beginning a new lifestyle can be really scary but physical and mental wellness is also very important.

- Reduced hour of sleep- Sleeping should last somewhat between 8-10 hours at night; this gives your mind a break and your body a chance to regenerate.
- Giving up too soon- I have seen people pick up this diet and after the first 2 weeks, they say "this diet isn't for me, I can't see the effect". Being on a diet is to create a long-lasting effect, so you have to be patient.
- Lacking on batch cooking- the key to success of any diet at all is preparation, if you have good food in your house, you will eat good food. If you don't, the probability of you eating out will increase. Meal prep and batch cooking will save you a whole lot of trouble.
- Sacrificing flavor and variety in meals- on of the major misconceptions about AIP diet is that you have to sacrifice flavor and diversity, I'm telling you: no way! Removing some foods doesn't mean we are removing all the foods. Spice it up! Mix up herbs! Be creative!
- Reintroducing food you cut out too quickly- the whole purpose of starting this diet is to give your body the time to heal and changes don't happen overnight. You need to give it time, perhaps before introducing those foods, consult with your nutrition therapist to figure out the best method.
- Avoid Isolation- the internet provides amazing support groups that offer guidance, be a part of that community to see how other people have done it.

AIP Diet versus the Paleo Piet

Yes, the two are much related but still different. Let's find out the difference.

- Paleo (short for paleolithic) diet is an eating plan that focuses on ingestion of nutrient dense food. It avoids processed food and "empty" calories. Dairy, legumes, grains are to be avoided. Quality meat, nuts, seeds, healthy fats, fruit and seafood should be eaten. Paleo diet essentially is just trying to get you to live like the cave men without the processed food so prevalent in our diet in the "modern" time.
- AIP diet sounds just about the same right? But it's not. AIP is stricter as it focus primarily on soothing inflammation and healing the gut and fighting the body-attacking antibodies. While Paleo for example allows nuts and seeds, AIP diet doesn't. In AIP diet, night shades aren't allowed either (they include tomatoes, peppers, potatoes). AIP is not permanent, it is usually recommended for about three or four months.

We are about to go into the cookbook proper, are you excited? I am!!....

Chapter 2
60 Amazing AIP Diet Recipes

We are here! About to wet your appetite, quite literally. This chapter will provide in sections 60 AIP diet recipes covering:

- AIP breakfast recipes
- AIP lunch recipes
- AIP dinner recipes
- AIP snacks and dessert recipes
- AIP drinks recipes

AIP Breakfast Recipes

It is widely known the most important meal of the day is the breakfast as is sets the body on the path of performing the activities for the day, kick off the day with these 12 amazing AIP recipes!

Apple-sage Pork Skillet

PREP TIME: 5 MINUTES, **COOK TIME**: 20 MINUTES

SERVES: 3-4 servings

INGREDIENTS:

- 1 lb. pastured ground pork
- 1 tablespoon apple cider vinegar
- 1 cup diced mushroom
- 2 tablespoon minced fresh sage
- Thinly sliced green onions
- 2 tablespoon coconut oil
- ½ diced white onion
- 1 diced medium white sweet potato
- 1 diced green apple
- ½ tablespoon sea salt

COOKING INSTRUCTIONS:

1. Place fresh coconut oil in the bottom of a heavy-bottomed skillet on medium-high heat. When the fat has melted, add the onion and cook. Stir for few minutes.
2. Turn down to medium heat and add the sweet potato. Cook for 4 minutes. Stir adding additional coconut oil if the mixture dries out and begins to stick.
3. Add the apple and cook for another 3 minutes. Stir occasionally. Add the mushrooms, sage and sea salt next, and cook until the sweet potatoes are soft. Turn off the stove, transfer to a medium sized bowl and set aside.
4. Add the ground pork to the same skillet you used for the vegetables. Turn the stove on to medium heat, break up all of the meat, and cook until no longer pink and lightly browned, stirring occasionally.
5. Add the apple and vegetable mixture back to the pan and add the vinegar. Stir to combine and turn off the stove.

NUTRITIONAL INFO:

Calories: 371, Total fat: 19 g, Saturated fat: 7.8 g, Carbohydrate: 22 g, Protein: 28 g, Sodium: 656 mg, Cholesterol: 89 mg, Dietary fibre: 3 g,

Fries with Bacon Chive Crumble

PREP TIME: 15 MINUTES, **COOK TIME:** 20 MINUTES
SERVES: 2 Servings

INGREDIENTS:

- 1 large white sweet potato, peeled and sliced into wide fries
- 2 large chopped zucchini
- 5 slices bacon
- 1 teaspoon lemon juice
- 2 cups thinly sliced curly kale
- 1 tablespoon chopped chives
- ½ teaspoon grated lemon zest
- ½ teaspoon minced garlic
- 1 teaspoon avocado oil
- ½ teaspoon sea salt

COOKING INSTRUCTIONS:

1. Preheat oven to 400°F. Arrange oven rack in the centre of the oven.
2. Toss sweet potato fries with avocado oil and sea salt on the baking sheet. Bake till the edges are lightly browned.

3. Cook bacon over medium heat until crispy on both sides. Transfer bacon to a cutting board, let cool and finely chop or crumble
4. Turn broiler on high and broil fries for 3 minutes, watching closely, until browned. Remove from oven and set aside.
5. Sautee zucchini in rendered bacon fat for 5 minutes over medium heat until lightly browned. Add kale to the pan and cook until bright green and tender.
6. Mix the crumbled or chopped bacon, chives, lemon zest, garlic and lemon juice together.
7. Divide the sweet potato fries among two plates. Add the green vegetables and sprinkle the bacon and chive crumbled on top. Sprinkle with additional lemon juice. Best serve warm.

NUTRITIONAL INFO:

Calories: 482, Total fat: 22 g, Saturated fat: 6.4 g, Carbohydrate: 38 g, Protein: 9.9 g, Sodium: 417 mg, Potassium: 565 mg, Cholesterol: 27 mg,

Moroccan Inspired Skillet

PREP TIME: 10 MINUTES, **COOK TIME:** 25 MINUTES
SERVES: 4 servings

INGREDIENTS:

- 1 lb. pastured ground pork
- 1 teaspoon ground turmeric
- ½ teaspoon sea salt
- ⅛ teaspoon cinnamon
- 1 teaspoon apple cider vinegar
- 1 medium diced sweet potato
- 1 small bunch chard, stems removed, separated and leaves chopped
- 3 cloves minced garlic
- ½ cup raisins
- 2 tablespoons coconut oil

COOKING INSTRUCTIONS:

1. Place the ground pork in the bottom of a cold heavy-bottomed pan and break up slightly with a kitchen knife. Turn on medium-high heat, and cook. Stir until the meat is browned and has absorbed all of the fat. Turn off the stove and transfer to a large bowl.

2. Place the same pan back on the stove, add the solid cooking fat and turn the heat to medium-high. Add the sweet potatoes and cook for five minutes after the fat has melted completely. Add the chard stems and cook for three more minutes.
3. Add the garlic, turmeric, sea salt, and cinnamon and stir to combine. Cook for a few more minutes until the sweet potatoes are soft.
4. Add the chard leaves, apple cider vinegar and raisins to the pan. Continue cooking until chard has wilted. Turn off the stove, salt and serve warm.

NUTRITIONAL INFO:

Calories: 967, Total fat: 12 g, Saturated fat: 4.6 g, Carbohydrate: 2 g, Protein: 28 g, Sugars: 2 g, Sodium: 430 mg, Cholesterol: 2 mg, Dietary fibre: 4 g

Porridge with Lemon and Berries

PREP TIME: 15 MINUTES, **COOK TIME**: 35 MINUTES
SERVES: 4 servings

INGREDIENTS:

- 1 large head cauliflower
- Handful mixed berries
- Toasted coconut chips
- ¾ cup finely shredded coconut
- Spoonful softly whipped coconut cream
- Zest of a large lemon
- Pinch salt
- 2 tablespoon coconut butter
- 3 cups coconut milk

COOKING INSTRUCTIONS:

1. Slice up the cauliflower into florets and put them into your food processor.
2. Pause for some time until the cauliflower is the same consistency as large grains of rice. Pulsing puts you in control.
3. Transfer the riced cauliflower to a pan, then add the remaining porridge ingredients and stir.

4. Bring up to a simmer, cover with a lid and cook for close to 30 minutes until the cauliflower is tender and the porridge nice.
5. Whip the coconut cream while the porridge is cooling. Start by removing your chilled coconut milk from the fridge.
6. Pour the thin coconut water into a jar.
7. Scoop out the cream and heat with a balloon whisk until soft peaks form.

NUTRITIONAL INFO:

Calories: 255, Total fat: 4 g, Saturated fat: 1.4 g, Carbohydrate: 17.3 g, Protein: 15 g, Sugar: 15 g, Sodium: 30 mg, Iron: 0.3 mg, Vitamin C: 2.5 mg, Dietary fibre: 4 g, Cholesterol: 85 mg,

Turkey Sausage

PREP TIME: 10 MINUTES, **COOK TIME**: 30 MINUTES
SERVES: 2 servings

INGREDIENTS:

- 1 pound of ground turkey
- 1 teaspoon sea salt
- 1 teaspoon fresh rosemary
- 1 teaspoon fresh thyme
- 2 tablespoons coconut oil
- ½ teaspoon garlic powder
- ½ teaspoon cinnamon
- 2 teaspoons fresh sage

COOKING INSTRUCTIONS:

1. Combine all ingredients except the oil and refrigerate for at least 30 minutes.
2. Add the oil and shape into patties of your choice. Cook in a lightly oiled skillet over medium heat until no longer pink in the middle.
3. Bake at 400°F for 25 minutes alternatively.
4. Serve hot.

NUTRITIONAL INFO:

Calories: 186, Total fat: 9.4 g, Saturated fat: 3.7 g, Carbohydrate: 2.5 g, Protein: 25.2 g, Sodium: 323 mg, Cholesterol: 87 mg, Dietary fibre: 3.2 g

Risotto with Greens

PREP TIME: 15 MINUTES, **COOK TIME**: 15 MINUTES
SERVES: 4 servings

INGREDIENTS:

- 1 pound of peeled butternut squash, cubed
- 1 teaspoon dried oregano
- ½ teaspoon onion powder
- ¼ teaspoon cinnamon
- ¼ teaspoon turmeric
- 1 tablespoon solid cooking fat
- 1 clove minced garlic
- 1 bunch rainbow chard, leaves cut into long ribbons and tough stems removed
- 1 teaspoon sea salt

COOKING INSTRUCTIONS:

1. Place squash in food processor and pulse for 45 seconds until squash is riced.
2. Heat solid cooking fat in a large skillet on medium-low heat. Add squash when fat has melted.

3. Cook and stir occasionally for 4-5 minutes. Add garlic, cook until fragrant.
4. Add remaining spices. Stir and cook 4-5 more minutes.
5. Add chard. Place lid over skillet for 2 minutes, allowing chard to wilt. Remove lid, stir to combine wilted chard.
6. Serve warm.

NUTRITIONAL INFO:

Calories: 259, Total fat: 7.8 g, Saturated fat: 2.5g, Carbohydrate: 25.5 g, Protein: 16.4 g, Sugar: 2.1 g, Sodium: 1306.3 mg, Potassium: 612.8 mg, Cholesterol: 16.7 mg, Dietary fibre: 2.5 g

Maple Sage Patties

PREP TIME: 10 MINUTES, **COOK TIME:** 10 MINUTES
SERVES: 8 servings

INGREDIENTS:

- 2 lbs pastured ground pork
- ½ teaspoon garlic powder
- 3 tablespoons minced fresh sage
- 1 teaspoon solid cooking fat
- 3 tablespoons grade B maple syrup
- ¾ teaspoon sea salt

COOKING INSTRUCTIONS:

1. Place the ground pork in a large mixing bowl and break into chunks with a wooden spoon. Drizzle the ground pork evenly with maple syrup and sprinkle with the sage, salt, and garlic powder.
2. Mix until thoroughly combined and form into patties.
3. Heat the solid cooking fat in a frying pan on medium heat. When the fat is melted and the pan is hot, add patties, cook 10 minutes a side, or until thoroughly cooked. Serve and enjoy.

NUTRITIONAL INFO:

Calories: 356, Total Fat: 28.2 g, Saturated fat: 7.9 g, Carbohydrate: 18.6 g, Protein: 32.2 g, Sodium: 784 mg, Cholesterol: 128 mg, Dietary fibre: 0.34 g,

Squash Browns

PREP TIME: 30 MINUTES, **COOK TIME**: 52 MINUTES
SERVES: 6 servings

INGREDIENTS:

- 1 medium spaghetti squash
- ½ cup and 2 tablespoons coconut oil, divided
- ½ teaspoon sea salt

COOKING INSTRUCTIONS:

1. Preheat the oven to 400 degrees Fahrenheit.
2. Brush each half of the squash with a tablespoon of oil and sprinkle with salt.
3. Bake until the squash easily pulls apart into spaghetti-like strands when scraped.
4. Allow the squash to cool, then shred it into strings and place the strings inside a colander. Squeeze the squash thoroughly.
5. Heat the ½ cup oil in a large skillet over medium-high heat. Shape a handful of spaghetti strings into a patty and add to the pan.
6. Fry until golden brown for 3- 4 minutes.
7. Flip and fry the other side, then remove from the skillet and drain on a paper towel.
8. Repeat for the remaining spaghetti squash.
9. Ready to be served.

NUTRITIONAL INFO:

Calories: 112, Total fat: 8 g, Saturated fat: 2.8 g, Carbohydrate: 47 g, Protein: 3 g, Sodium: 546 mg, Cholesterol: 38 mg, Dietary fibre: 1 g

Italian Spiced 50/50 Sausages

PREP TIME: 20 MINUTES, **COOK TIME:** 20 MINUTES
SERVES: 7-10 servings

INGREDIENTS:

- 1 pound of grass-fed ground beef
- ½ teaspoon sea salt
- 1 tablespoon minced fresh thyme
- 1 tablespoon solid cooking fat(lard, coconut oil)
- ½ teaspoon garlic powder
- 1 pound of pastured ground pork
- 1 tablespoon minced fresh oregano

COOKING INSTRUCTIONS:

1. Place the ground beef, pork, herbs, garlic powder and salt in a large bowl and combine well with your hands. Form into 7 or more patties and place on a plate.
2. Heat the solid cooking fat in a frying pan on medium heat. Add patties when the fat is melted. Cook until thoroughly cooked. You may have to do this in two batches.

NUTRITIONAL INFO:

Calories: 532, Total fat: 17 g, Saturated fat: 5.1 g, Carbohydrate: 7.3 g, Protein: 22.3 g, Sodium: 770 mg, Cholesterol: 25 mg, Dietary fibre: 4.2 g

Plantain Wrap

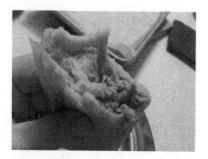

PREP TIME: 10 MINUTES, **COOK TIME:** 30 MINUTES
SERVES: 6 pieces

INGREDIENTS:

- 3 Green Plantains
- 1/3 cup extra virgin olive oil
- 1 teaspoon sea salt
- 1 cup of water

COOKING INSTRUCTIONS:

1. Peel and chop green plantains.
2. Puree the plantains as much as you can in your food processor.
3. Add the remaining ingredients and puree for a minute or two.
4. Scrape down the sides so any larger chunks get incorporated.
5. Spread onto a parchment lined sheet tray.
6. Bake at 375°F for about 25-30 minutes.
7. Cut into 6 pieces and serve with yummy food.

NUTRITIONAL INFO:

Calories: 212, Total fat: 1.8 g, Saturated fat: 0.3 g, Carbohydrate:48 g, Protein: 3 g, Sugar: 13 g, Sodium: 260 mg, Dietary fibre: 4 g, Potassium: 739 mg, Vitamin C: 27 mg, Cholesterol: 0.9 mg

Banana Bread

PREP TIME: 10 MINUTES, **COOK TIME:** 25 MINUTES
SERVES: 16 slices

INGREDIENTS:

- 1 cup of mashed ripe bananas
- ½ teaspoon baking soda
- 1 tablespoon honey
- 1 teaspoon vanilla
- 1 ½ teaspoons lemon juice
- ¼ cup coconut flour
- ½ cup arrowroot starch
- ½ teaspoon salt
- ½ teaspoon cinnamon
- ¼ cup of melted coconut oil
- ½ cup of softened coconut butter

COOKING INSTRUCTIONS:

1. Preheat oven to 350°F.
2. Grease pan with coconut oil.
3. Mix wet ingredients in mixer until smooth.
4. Mix dry ingredients together in a bowl.

5. Pour dry mixture into wet ingredients and mix until combined.
6. Spread into prepared pan.
7. Bake for 25-30 minutes.
8. Yummy banana bread is ready to serve.

NUTRITIONAL INFO:

Calories: 185, Total fat: 23.2 g, Saturated fat: 4.6 g, Carbohydrates: 16.1 g, Protein: 4.8 g, Sugar: 6.1 g, Sodium: 743 mg, Cholesterol: 62.8 mg, Dietary fibre: 4.4 g, Vitamin C: 14 mg

Sticky Buns

PREP TIME: 10 MINUTES, **COOK TIME**: 35 MINUTES
SERVES: 6 servings

INGREDIENTS:

- ¼ cup of maple syrup
- 1/3 cup + 2 tablespoon coconut flour
- 1/3 cup of coconut oil
- 1 tablespoon vanilla
- 1 tablespoon coconut oil reserve to end
- 2 tablespoon maple syrup(reserve to end)
- 1/3 teaspoon baking powder

INSTRUCTIONS:

1. Pre-heat oven to 350°F and put cupcake tins into the pan.
2. Add coconut oil, vanilla, baking powder and maple syrup to a medium sized bowl and mix well with electric beaters.
3. Add the coconut flour few scoops at a time and mix well.
4. Scoop batter evenly between 6 cupcake tins.
5. Bake for about 20 minutes or until toothpick comes out clean.
6. Let the muffins cool while you make the topping. Add the reserved coconut oil and maple syrup to a pot and stir while it comes to a boil.
7. Pour the syrup mixture evenly over the muffins and stick the whole tray in the freezer for 10-15 minutes to harden.

NUTRITIONAL INFO:

Calories: 275, Total fat: 1.5 g, Saturated fat: 0.7 g, Carbohydrates: 52 g, Protein: 45 g, Sugar: 2 g, Iron: 5.2 mg, Magnesium: 153 mg, Dietary fibre: 5.3 g, Cholesterol: 12 mg

AIP Lunch Recipes

Certainly, breakfast is widely accepted as the most important meal of the day but its energy wanes off mostly at the middle of a hectic workday. Hence, the energy level needs to rise again which can only be done by a call on Lunch i.e. afternoon meal.

For a person on Autoimmune paleo (AIP) diet, the health of the individual is paramount hence, all lunch is not meant for the person but a well-structured lunch that continues the diet scheme from breakfast should be taken.

This section is dedicated to 13 awesome Autoimmune paleo lunch, their recipes, preparation and supportive images.

Here we go!

AIP Salads

Calamari Summer Salad

PREP TIME: 30 MINUTES, **COOK TIME:** 3 MINUTES
SERVES: 4 servings

INGREDIENTS:

- ½ fennel bulb, a very thin slice
- ½ cup chopped, fresh parsley, basil and chives
- ½ cup plus one tablespoon Olive oil
- 1 lemon zest
- 1 very thin sliced zucchini(small)
- 1 small yellow summer squash (sliced very thin)
- 1 tablespoon minced shallot
- 3 tablespoons red wine vinegar
- 4 red radishes (sliced very thin)
- 12 Kalamata olives, sliced in half
- 12 oz. squid, cleaned, body sliced into rings tentacles left whole.

COOKING INSTRUCTIONS:

1. Get a large bowl and place the radish, zucchini, squash and fennel inside of it and set aside

2. Shake a mixture of vinegar, lemon, shallot, and ½ cup of olive oil vigorously in a glass jar for about 2 minutes
3. Combine the remaining tablespoon of oil, ¼ cup of water in a large skillet, bring over moderate heat to simmer and add the squid then cover for about 2-3 minutes. Make the squid opaque by poaching it.
4. Mix squid, herbs and olives into vegetables. Pour over and mix well, with salt added to best of taste

NUTRITIONAL INFO:

Calories: 229, Total fat: 15.9 g, Saturated fat: 4.6 g, Carbohydrate: 3.1 g, Protein: 17.8 g, Potassium: 306.3 mg, Dietary fibre: 0.1 g, Sodium: 50.9 mg, Cholesterol: 264.1 mg

Shrimp Salad with Cilantro-Lemon Ranch Dressing

PREP TIME: 5 MINUTES, **COOK TIME:** 5 MINUTES
SERVES: 2 servings

INGREDIENTS:

- 1 tablespoon coconut oil
- 12 ounces peeled, deveined shrimp
- ½ head romaine, shredded
- 1 carrot, grated
- ½ green apple, cored and chopped into chunks
- 1 avocado, pitted and chopped into chunks
- 1-2 tablespoons cilantro, for garnish

COOKING INSTRUCTIONS:

1. Place the coconut oil in the bottom of a skillet on medium heat. When the fat has melted and the pan is hot, saute the shrimp in batches, making sure not to crowd, and cooking for 1-2 minutes or until opaque and fully cooked. Remove and set aside to cool.
2. Place the romaine, grated carrot, green apple, avocado, and cilantro in a large bowl with the shrimp. Arrange, or toss to combine.
3. Serve with cilantro-lemon ranch dressing.

NUTRITIONAL INFO:

Calories: 496, Total fat: 25.3 g, Saturated fat: 8.8 g, Carbohydrate: 34.6 g, Protein: 35.9 g, Sodium: 358.9 mg, Sugar: 4.7 g, Cholesterol: 82.8 mg, Dietary fibre: 13.7 g

Carrot, Cucumber, and Avocado Salad

PREP TIME: 35 MIN, **COOK TIME**: 2 HOURS
SERVES: 4 servings

INGREDIENTS:

- 1/4 cup apple cider vinegar
- 1/2 inch piece of ginger, grated fine
- 1lb pickling cucumber (sliced thin) with a mandoline
- 1 lb. rainbow carrots, length (half) and cut into 3-inch chunks
- 1 teaspoon sea salt
- 1 avocado, cubed
- 1 bunch cilantro, chopped
- 2 tablespoons honey

COOKING INSTRUCTIONS:

1. Mix together vigorously the honey and cider vinegar in a small bowl until they combine
2. Pour over the cucumber slices, sprinkle whit sea salt and ginger, and stir to combine. This mixture should be placed in the refrigerator overnight or at least 2-hours

3. When you are ready to make your salad, boil a large quantity of water in a large pot on the stovetop (or any other alternative. Blanch the carrots for 3-4 minutes, and then rinse with cold water
4. Strain the cucumber mixture, reserving some of the juice to add back to the salad
5. Get a neat large bowl, add the avocado, carrots, cilantro and cucumber mixture to a large bowl and toss to combine. Some of the cucumber juice can then be added with Olive oil to taste.
6. It's ready to be served!

NUTRITIONAL INFO:

Calories: 90, Total fat: 4.6 g, Saturated fat: 1.8 g, Carbohydrate: 10.7 g, Protein: 3.3 g, Sodium: 110.7 mg, Potassium: 341.7 mg, Cholesterol: 8.3 mg, Dietary fibre: 2.5 g

Deli-Style Italian Pasta Salad

PREP TIME: 10 MINUTES

SERVES: 4 servings

INGREDIENTS:

- 4 cups of packed raw zucchini noodles
- ¼ teaspoon dried dill
- ½ cup of quartered and sliced red onion
- ¼ cup of extra virgin olive oil
- ¼ teaspoon fine sea salt
- 14 oz. can quartered artichoke hearts
- 2 tablespoons balsamic vinegar
- ½ cup of pitted black kalamata olives
- ½ teaspoon dried oregano flakes

COOKING INSTRUCTIONS:

1. Toss the zucchini noodles, artichoke hearts, black kalamata olives and the sliced red onions together in a large bowl.
2. Whisk the extra virgin olive oil, balsamic vinegar, oregano flakes, dried dill and sea salt together in a glass measuring cup to make the dressing.
3. Toss the dressing with the pasta salad until evenly coated.
4. Serve immediately or store in the refrigerator for up to 24 hours and serve cold.

NUTRITIONAL INFO:

Calories: 79, Total fat: 12.7 g, Saturated fat: 4.8 g, Carbohydrate: 14.3 g, Protein: 5.1 g, Potassium: 567.4 mg, Sodium:87.7 mg, Cholesterol: 9.1 mg, Dietary fibre: 4.3 g

Chicken Vegetable Salad

PREP TIME: 10 MINUTES, **COOK TIME:** 20 MINUTES
SERVES: 2 servings

INGREDIENTS:

- 2 Tablespoons of olive oil
- 1 sliced pickled beetroot
- ½ sliced onion
- 60 ml avocado oil, to cook with
- 1 teaspoon turmeric
- 1 tablespoon of onion powder
- 1 tablespoon of garlic powder
- 2 cups salad leaves, washed
- 1 sliced cucumber
- Parsley for garnish
- 15 ml Tablespoon of lemon juice
- 2 chicken breasts, cut into cubes
- 1/2 teaspoon dried oregano
- Salt to taste

INSTRUCTIONS:

1. Mix the olive oil and lemon juice in a small bowl. Season with salt and set aside.

2. Mix together the turmeric powder, onion powder, garlic powder, and dried oregano. Season with salt and drop the chicken pieces into the bowl to coat.
3. Heat the avocado oil in a pan and cook the chicken until they are done. Remove from the heat and set aside.
4. Toss the salad leaves and cucumber in the salad dressing and top with the cooked chicken pieces. Add the beetroot, onion slices, and parsley.

NUTRITIONAL INFO:

Calories: 716, Total fat: 49 g, Saturated fat: 14 g, Carbohydrate: 18 g, Protein: 51 g, Sodium: 687 mg, Sugar: 9 g, Dietary fibre: 4 g, Cholesterol: 98 mg

AIP Pork, Beef, and Chicken
Orange-Glazed Pork Tenderloin

PREP TIME: 8 HOURS, **COOK TIME:** 1 HOUR
SERVES: 4 servings

INGREDIENTS:

- 1/6 cup of coconut aminos
- 1/6 cup of honey
- 1/6 cup of orange marmalade or 1 tablespoon each of orange Zest, orange juice, and honey
- 1 pound of pork tenderloin
- 2 stalks green onions, sliced
- 2 teaspoon white wine vinegar

COOKING INSTRUCTIONS:

1. All ingredients except the green onion are combined in an oven safe, lidded dish and marinate in the fridge overnight
2. Preheat the oven to 350 degrees Fahrenheit (350^{0}F)
3. The tenderloin should be baked uncovered for 1 hour in the oven, or until the internal temperature reaches 145 degrees (145^{0}F)
4. Serve garnished with the green onion.

NUTRITIONAL INFO:

Calories: 231, Total fat: 10.2 g, Saturated fat: 3.6 g, Carbohydrate: 15 g, Protein: 21 g, Sugar: 31.3 g, Sodium: 320.6 mg, Potassium: 412.8 mg, Dietary fibre: 0.9 g, Vitamin C: 78 mg, Cholesterol: 89.5 mg

Grilled Chicken Thighs with Pineapple Mint Salsa

PREP TIME: 10 MIN, **COOK TIME**: 35 MIN.
SERVES: 6 servings

INGREDIENTS:

For the Chicken:
- ½ tablespoon sea salt
- ½ tablespoon ginger powder
- ½ tablespoon garlic powder
- 3 lbs. bone-in, skin-on chicken thighs

For the Salsa:
- ½ large pineapple, cut into half inch chunks
- ½ tablespoon sea salt
- ½ tablespoon lemon, juice
- ½ tablespoon ginger powder
- 1 avocado, cut into 1/2-inch chunks
- 1 oz. fresh mint leaves, finely chopped
- 1 clove garlic, minced
- 1 bunch radishes, tops removed and cut into ½ inch chunks
- 1 bunch green onions, root and top ends removed and finely chopped

COOKING INSTRUCTIONS:

1. The grill is first pre-heated
2. The spices and salt are combined in a small bowl and set aside.

3. The chicken should be thoroughly dried by using a piece of paper towel and set aside while you warm the grill
4. The chicken should be covered with the spice mixture by using the figure to rub thoroughly, after which it should be cooked
5. When the grill is ensured hot, the chicken is placed skin-side down and cooking is carried on for 5-7 minutes (this cooking can stop when the skin start getting crispy). The chicken should be flipped over and cooked until thermometer reads 165^0 F or it can be cooked for another 5-7 minutes.
6. The salsa ingredients are combined and stirred gently until properly combined.
7. The chicken can then be served with salsa on top

NUTRITIONAL INFO:

Calories: 780, Total fat: 25.4 g, Saturated fat: 6.3 g, Carbohydrate: 82.7 g, Protein: 50.9 g, Sugar: 2 g, Sodium: 1107.5 mg, Potassium: 452.6 mg, Calcium: 53 mg, Magnesium: 26 mg, Dietary fibre: 2.7 g, Vitamin C: 26 mg, Cholesterol: 178.6 mg

Zuppa Toscana

PREP TIME: 5 MINUTES, **COOK TIME:** 25 MINUTES
SERVES: 6 servings

INGREDIENTS:

- 1/3 cup of coconut milk
- 1 small onion, chopped
- 1 large celeriac, peeled and chopped
- 1 lb. ground beef
- 2 cups of kale, chopped
- 2 cloves garlic, minced
- 4 cups of bone broth
- 6 slices bacon

COOKING INSTRUCTIONS:

1. The bacon should be cooked in a stock pot over a medium heat until crispy. The bacon should be removed while the bacon fat is left behind in the pot.
2. The bacon is cooked with onion added for about 3 minutes or translucent.
3. Then add the ground beef and cook, and stir until it's brown for about 3 minutes.
4. Garlic is also added, cooked and stirred for 2-3 minutes.
5. Add the broth and celeriac and boil.
6. The celeriac is made tendered by 20 minutes of simmered and uncovered cooking
7. Add the coconut milk and kale and cook until the kale wilts.
8. The meal is served with crumbled bacon.

NUTRITIONAL INFO:

Calories: 323, Total fat: 4 g, Saturated fat: 1.8 g, Carbohydrate: 10.3 g, Protein: 16.4 g, Sodium: 960 mg, Dietary fibre: 2 g, Cholesterol: 32 mg

AIP Fish and Seafood

Honey-Lemon Glazed Salmon

PREP TIME: 10 MINUTES, **COOK TIME:** 10 MINUTES
SERVES: 4 servings

INGREDIENTS:

- ¼ cup of honey
- 1 teaspoon lemon zest
- 1 teaspoon fish sauce
- 1 teaspoon sea salt, divided
- 1 ½ pounds wild salmon, skin-on, cut into 4 to 5 even filets
- 2 minced garlic cloves
- 2 tablespoons cassava flour
- 2 tablespoons avocado oil

COOKING INSTRUCTIONS:

1. Mix together vigorously together the garlic, lemon juice, honey, lemon zest and ½ teaspoon sea salt in a glass bowl (or any other alternatives).
2. Coat both sides of a dry salmon (by patting) filets evenly with cassava flour and remaining ½ teaspoon sea salt.
3. Heat avocado oil in a large cast iron skillet over medium-high heat. Sear the salmon, flesh side down, for 2 minutes until browned. Flip with a large spatula and sear skin side down for 2 minutes until browned

4. Pour in the glaze and allow it to bubble and froth. Continue to cook the salmon skin side down for 2 more minutes as the glaze reduces. Flip one last time and reduce heat to medium-low.
5. Finish cooking the salmon flesh side down as the glaze caramelizes for 2 more minutes and the fish is cooked throughout.
6. Transfer to a serving platter and spoon any leftover glaze onto the salmon prior to serving.

NUTRITIONAL INFO:

Calories: 277, Total fat: 11.2 g, Saturated fat: 3.9 g, Carbohydrate: 21.3 g, Protein: 25.7 g, Sugar: 17.5 g, Sodium: 844 .2 mg, Potassium: 84 mg, Dietary fibre: 0.7 g, Cholesterol: 60 mg

Wild Salmon with Zucchini Noodles

PREP TIME: 10 MINUTES, **COOK TIME**: 10 MINUTES.
SERVES: 4 servings

INGREDIENTS:

- 1 lb fillet wild sockeye salmon, skin on
- 1 teaspoon olive oil
- 2-3 large yellow zucchini, spiralled into spaghetti-sized noodles
- Large handful baby salad leaves (I love tatsoi, arugula for this)
- Edible flowers or petals (optional)
- For the dressing:
- 3 oz (3 tightly packed cups) basil, thinner stalks included
- $3/4$ cup of mild olive oil
- 2 garlic cloves, roughly chopped
- 2 anchovy fillets (from a can)
- 1-1½ teaspoon lemon juice
- Generous pinch sea salt

COOKING INSTRUCTIONS:

1. Put the salmon onto a baking tray, skin side up, and broil for around 5 minutes until just cooked through. The exact time will depend on how thick your fillet is.
2. Allow to cool enough so you don't burn your fingers, then peel off the skin and break the flesh up into large flakes.

3. Meanwhile, heat the olive oil in a large sauté pan and add the noodles. Gently toss them around for 3 minutes or until semi-softened and warmed through. Turn off the heat, set a colander over a lipped plate and tip the noodles inside. Put into a warm place and allow the noodles to drain off their excess liquid whilst the fish cooks.
4. To make the dressing, put the appropriate ingredients into a blender and whizz until smooth and thick. Taste and add more lemon juice, salt or other ingredients as desired. Don't forget the flavor will be diluted somewhat when it is mixed in with everything else.
5. Put the zucchini noodles into a large bowl and add the baby leaves and salmon. Add as much of the dressing as you like and gently mix, allowing the leaves to wilt in the bowl. Serve garnished with basil and edible flowers for a bit of pretty.

NUTRITIONAL INFO:

Calories: 65, Total fat: 5.1 g, Saturated fat: 1.8 g, Carbohydrate: 2 g, Protein: 35 g, Sodium:600.7 mg, Potassium: 407.4 mg, Iron: 2.7 mg Vitamin D: 6.1 mg, Cholesterol: 9 mg, Dietary fibre: 2.4g

Crispy Drill Fried Fish

PREP TIME: 1 HOUR, **COOK TIME:** 20 MINUTES
SERVES: 2 servings

INGREDIENTS:
- 1 lb. firm, white fish
- 2 cups of sauerkraut juice
- ¾ cup of tapioca flour, divided
- ¼ cup of water
- 1 teaspoon sea salt
- 1½ teaspoon dried dill
- 1 cup of palm shortening

COOKING INSTRUCTIONS:
1. Cut fish into approximately 1-2-inch pieces. Pour sauerkraut juice into a gallon-sized sealable plastic bag, add fish. Marinate in refrigerator for 1 hour.
2. Turn oven broiler to low, adjust oven rack close to element.
3. Drain fish. In shallow dish, stir ¼ cup flour with ¼ cup water until flour dissolves. In separate shallow dish, mix remaining flour, salt, and dill.
4. Using a heavy-bottomed pot or frying pan, bring shortening to approximately 350 degrees F.
5. Dredge fish in liquid mixture. Repeat in dill mixture to coat. Shake off excess flour.

6. Carefully place fish into oil, being sure not to crowd the pan. Fry 1 minute per side, using tongs to flip fish.
7. Remove to paper towelled lined plate. When oil is drained, place fish on baking sheet, place under oven broiler for 2 minutes (use a timer!).
8. While fish is under broiler, fry next batch and drain. Take fish out of oven, repeat frying for 30 seconds to 1 minute per side or until golden brown and very crisp. Remove to paper towel lined plate until oil is drained.
9. Repeat with remaining batches.
10. Serve immediately while still very hot.

NUTRITIONAL INFO:

Calories: 211, Total fat: 11.2 g, Saturated fat: 3.6 g, Carbohydrate: 15.4 g, Protein: 13.3 g, Sodium: 484.1 mg, Dietary fibre: 0.5 g, Cholesterol: 30.9 mg

Avocado Green Smoothie

PREP TIME: 5 MINUTES

SERVES: 1 glass

INGREDIENTS:
- ½ ripe avocado
- 1 handful of greens of your choice (kale, chard, spinach)
- 1 cup of ice
- 1 ripe banana
- ½ cup of coconut milk

INSTRUCTIONS:
1. Place the avocado, banana, and ice into the blender.
2. Top with the greens (kale, chard, spinach).
3. Blend until smooth (add extra coconut milk if needed).

NUTRITIONAL INFO:

Calories: 266, Total fat: 15 g, Saturated fat: 4.3 g, Carbohydrate: 36.7 g, Protein: 3 g, Sugar: 15.1 g, Potassium: 487 mg, Dietary fibre: 8.8 g, Cholesterol: 23 mg, Calcium: 18.8 mg

Stuffed Chicken Breast

PREP TIME: 20 MINUTES, **COOK TIME:** 20 MINUTES
SERVES: 2 servings

INGREDIENTS:
- 80 ml olive oil
- 50 g basil leaves
- 2 roughly chopped cloves garlic
- ½ lemon, zest and juice
- 2 chicken breasts (approx. 200 g each)
- Salt, to taste
- 30 ml avocado oil, to cook chicken in
- 300 g of cauliflower broken into florets

INSTRUCTIONS:
1. Make the pesto by blitzing the olive oil, basil leaves, and garlic with the zest and juice of half a lemon using a mini food processor. Season with salt.
2. Preheat the oven to 350°F.
3. Place the cauliflower florets into a microwave and cook until tender. Remove and mash well until smooth. Stir in 2 tablespoons of the pesto and set aside.
4. Season chicken breasts with salt and make a deep cut in one side of each chicken breast.
5. Add 2 tablespoons of avocado to a frying pan and fry on the chicken breast on both sides until golden. Remove from the heat and place on a work surface. It

will still be fairly raw on the inside so be mindful of the utensils and your work surface.
6. Once the chicken is cool enough to handle, spoon the creamy cauli-pesto mixture into the pocket of each chicken breast, then place on a roasting tray and place in the oven for an additional 20 minutes until the chicken has sufficiently cooked through.
7. Serve with side salad or a baked sweet potato.

NUTRITIONAL INFO:
Calories: 661, Total fat: 48 g, Saturated fat: 12.3 g, Carbohydrate: 8 g, Protein: 50 g, sugar: 4 g, Sodium: 546 mg, Dietary fibre: 4 g, Cholesterol: 132 mg

AIP Dinner Recipes

You didn't think I was going to let you go to bed hungry, did you? I have got another awesome 15 dinner recipes! Enjoy!

Shrimp Scampi

PREP TIME: 5 MINUTES, COOK TIME: 10 MINUTES
SERVES: 4-6 servings

INGREDIENTS:
- ¼ cup of avocado oil
- 2 lb. shrimp, peeled and deveined
- 1 tablespoon sea salt
- 1½ tablespoons fresh or dried parsley
- 5 cloves minced garlic
- 2 tablespoon lemon juice
- 1 teaspoon fresh lemon zest
- ½ cup of dry white wine

COOKING INSTRUCTIONS:
1. Heat oil over medium heat
2. Pour the shrimp to the hot oil and cook for about 3 minutes. Season with sea salt

3. Stir garlic into the shrimp and cook for about 3 minutes
4. Remove cooked shrimp and transfer to a bowl
5. Add lemon juice and white wine to the pan
6. Simmer for about 2 minutes
7. Remove from heat and mix together vigorously the remaining ingredients into the sauce
8. Add the shrimp back into the hot pan and serve

NUTRITIONAL INFO:

Calories: 762, Total fat: 26.9 g, Saturated fat: 8.6 g, Carbohydrate: 0.02 g, Protein: 28.7 mg, Sugar: 0.02 g, Sodium: 1260 mg, Cholesterol: 417 mg

Pumpkin Chili

PREP TIME: 10 MINUTES. **COOK TIME:** 25 MINUTES.
SERVES: 2 servings

INGREDIENTS:
- 1 lb. grass-fed ground beef
- ½ cup of chopped carrot
- 3 tablespoon coconut oil
- 1 tablespoon garlic powder
- 15 oz organic pureed pumpkin
- 1 small diced onion
- 1 tablespoon ground turmeric
- 1 tablespoon sea salt
- 1 tablespoon dried oregano
- 1 tablespoon ground cinnamon
- ½ tablespoon ground cloves
- ½ cup of pastured bone broth
- 3 cloves chopped garlic
- 2 cups of fresh spinach

COOKING INSTRUCTIONS:
1. Sauté coconut oil, onions and carrots for about 3-5 minutes in a large sauce pan
2. Add garlic and sauté for 2 minutes
3. Add ground beef, break up and brown for 3 minutes
4. Add pureed pumpkin, vinegar, apple cider, broth and other seasonings. Cover and simmer for about 8-10 minutes

5. Add spinach to chilli mix, stir and simmer for 3-5 minutes

NUTRITIONAL INFO:
Calories: 642, Total fat: 7.8 g, Saturated fat: 2.3 g, Carbohydrate: 20.1 g, Protein: 15.7 g, Sugar: 9.5 g, Sodium: 438 mg, Dietary fibre: 4.5 g, Cholesterol: 35 mg

Creamy Garlic Spaghetti Squash Casserole

PREP TIME: 5 MINUTES, **COOK TIME:** 55 MINUTES
SERVES: 6 servings

INGREDIENTS:
- 1 medium spaghetti squash
- 1 lb. sausage
- 2 cups of diced mushroom
- 2 tablespoon minced garlic
- 16 oz. coconut milk
- 1 tablespoon salt
- 1 tablespoon pepper
- 4 cups of broccoli florets
- ¼ cup of arrowroot flour

COOKING INSTRUCTIONS:
1. Preheat oven to 400° Fahrenheit
2. Slice spaghetti squash and scoop the seeds. Place the two halves face-down on a baking sheet and place in the oven to bake for about 25-30 minutes
3. While cooking the squash, add sausage to a large pan and cook for about 8-10 minutes. Remove from the pan and reserve 1 tablespoon of fat in the pan
4. Remove squash from oven and set aside
5. Prepare the creamy garlic sauce. Add mushrooms and cook until they soften. Add in the arrowroot flour and minced garlic and mix with mushrooms for about 2 minutes

6. Add coconut milk and stir for 2 minutes. Use a mix together vigorously to mix if needed. The sauce will bubble.
7. After few minutes, turn heat down and simmer
8. Add the cooked sausage, creamy garlic sauce and broccoli and mix properly
9. Now to be served

NUTRITIONAL INFO:

Calories: 653, Total fat: 3.2 g, Saturated fat: 0.9 g, Carbohydrate: 65.1 g, Protein: 21.6 g, Dietary fibre: 2.1 g, Cholesterol: 15 mg

Mini Lasagna

PREP TIME: 15 MIN. **COOK TIME**: 5 MIN.
SERVES: 2 servings

INGREDIENTS:
- 1 large zucchini
- 1 cup of fresh basil leaves
- 2 garlic cloves
- 2 tablespoon red wine vinegar
- Olive oil
- 1 tablespoon bacon fat
- 2 cups of cauliflower alfredo sauce
- 1 lb ground lamb
- 1 tablespoon dried Italian herb
- 2 portobello mushrooms
- 1 tablespoon salt

COOKING INSTRUCTIONS:
1. Preheat the oven to 400°F
2. Slice vegetables into thin slices. Cut zucchini to thin rounds. Slice Portobello mushroom into thin rounds
3. Heat a large skillet on medium heat, add in fat and minced garlic cloves. Then add in the ground lamb. Add salt and herbs. Cook for about two minutes.
4. Add vinegar and keep stirring until well browned, then remove from heat.
5. Drizzle little olive oil then add Portobello slice to the bottom, add salt. Put little lamb, some alfredo sauce then add in some fresh basils
6. Layer the zucchini rounds over the lamb. Sprinkle little salt and add in another layer of Portobello. Then some more alfredo, lamb and zucchini. Put little salt, basil and olive oil. Repeat with the next ramekin
7. Tower lasagna outside of ramekin before baking
8. Place the ramekin in the oven and roast for 50 minutes
9. Remove from oven and allow it to cool
10. Garnish with extra basil and serve warm

NUTRITIONAL INFO:

Calories: 257, Total fat: 14.3 g, Saturated fat: 6.1 g, Carbohydrate: 12.7 g, Protein: 18.4 g, Sugar:1.2 g, Sodium: 452 mg, Dietary fibre: 0.6 g, Cholesterol: 59 mg

Chicken Salsa Verde Tacos

PREP TIME: 15 MINUTES, **COOK TIME:** 25 MINUTES
SERVES: 6 servings

INGREDIENTS:
- 1 packed cup finely sliced red onions
- Fine sea salt
- 170g cooked chicken, chopped
- ¼ cup and 2 tablespoon fresh lemon juice
- ½ cup nightshade free roasted green onion salsa verde
- Sliced avocado
- 1 batch of foolproof grain tortillas
- Coconut yoghurt
- 3 cups coleslaw mix

COOKING INSTRUCTIONS:
1. Finely slice the onions. Add the sliced onion to a bowl along with the lemon juice and salt. Toss to coat them in the lemon mixture. Sit for about 10-15 minutes, tossing every 5 minutes until the onions begin to soften. Transfer the onions and all the liquid to a jar.
2. Add the chopped chicken to a small saucepan, along with the Roasted Green Onion Salsa Verde and a couple of splashes of chicken broth. Stir to combine, then add additional salt, to taste. Warm the chicken over medium low heat until thoroughly reheated, but don't allow the pan to dry out. Add a little extra chicken broth.
3. Once the skillet is hot, add the tortillas to reheat, flipping to the other side once the tortilla is warm and crisp to the touch.

4. When both sides are hot and have some nice golden brown – or even char – marks, transfer to a cloth lined surface so that they keep warm, but don't become soggy. Repeat until all of the tortillas are done.
5. Once the chicken is reheated thoroughly, your tacos are ready to assemble. Transfer the warmed tortillas to plates, then top each one with some of the coleslaw mix. Use two forks to divide the chicken evenly between the tacos — you don't want to bring too much cooking liquid with the meat, or the tacos will be soggy. Top the salsa Verde chicken with some of the lemon pickled onions.

NUTRITIONAL INFO:

Calories: 712, Total fat: 21 g, Saturated fat: 6.3g, Carbohydrate: 56.3 g, Protein: 13 g, Sodium: 637.5 mg, Calcium:12 mg, Vitamin C: 3 mg, Dietary fibre: 8.9 g, Cholesterol:7 g

Italian Calzone

PREP TIME: 10 MIN. **COOK TIME:** 40 MIN.
SERVES: 1 serving

INGREDIENTS:
- 1 cup of cooked, mashed, and cooled white sweet potato
- ⅓ cup of arrowroot starch
- ½ cup of diced fully cooked AIP-compliant sausage, ham, or pancetta
- ¼ cup of sliced green or black olives
- ¼ teaspoon sea salt
- 1 garlic clove, minced
- ½ teaspoon dried Italian herb seasoning
- Small handful baby spinach
- 1 teaspoon olive oil

COOKING INSTRUCTIONS:
1. Preheat the oven to 375°F. Line a baking sheet with parchment paper.
2. Combine the sweet potato, arrowroot starch and sea salt until fully combined in a food processor.
3. Spoon the dough onto the prepared baking sheet. Place extra sheet of parchment on top of the dough and use it to assist you in shaping the dough into an 8-inch diameter circle.
4. Distribute the sausage, olives, garlic, seasoning, and spinach evenly on one half of the circle. Use the bottom piece of parchment paper to assist in folding the other half of the dough on top of the filling to form the calzone.
5. Brush the olive oil all over the calzone.
6. Use a fork and the help your fingers to gently seal the dough.

7. Bake the calzone for about 28 to 30 minutes until the edges are lightly golden brown. Turn the broiler on high and broil for 2 to 4 minutes until the top of the calzone is a golden brown and crispy in spots.
8. Let cool for about 5-7 minutes before slicing.

NUTRITIONAL INFO:
Calories: 832, Total fat: 34 g, Saturated fat: 5.6 g, Carbohydrate: 54.9 g, Protein: 36.1 g, Sodium: 1960 mg, Dietary fibre: 2 g, Cholesterol: 85 mg

Hearty Salmon Chowder

PREP TIME: 10 MIN. **COOK TIME:** 45 MIN.
SERVES: 4-6 servings

INGREDIENTS:
- 2 tablespoon solid fat
- 1 small fennel, thinly sliced, fronds reserved
- 1 large thinly sliced leek
- 2 sliced stalks celery
- 1 small celeriac, peeled and cut into ¼ inch diced
- 2 small rutabaga, peeled and cut into 1/2 inch cubes
- 2 large carrots, cut into 1/2 inch cubes
- 3 sprigs fresh thyme
- 3/4 lb. (340g) wild salmon fillet, skin on
- 2 cups (500ml) of coconut milk
- 1 cup (250ml) of chicken or fish bone broth
- 1 large bay leaf
- 3/4 teaspoon sea salt, or to taste
- chopped curly parsley to garnish

COOKING INSTRUCTIONS:

1. Melt fat in a large pan and add the vegetables and thyme. Put the lid on the pan and cook for about 25-30 minutes.
2. Stir once in a while.
3. Place the salmon skin side down into a large sauté pan with the coconut milk, broth and bay leaf. Bring the liquid to a gentle simmer and poach the fish for about 6-8 minutes until only just cooked.
4. Remove the salmon from the coconut milk, discard the skin and bay leaf.
5. Pour the milk into the pan with the vegetables; bring up to a simmer and cook a further 5 minutes or until the rutabaga and carrots has cooked through. Flake the salmon into large pieces, add to the vegetables and reheat, being careful not to let the chowder boil. Add sea salt to taste.
6. Serve with the reserved fennel fronds and chopped parsley on the top.

NUTRITIONAL INFO:

Calories: 360, Total fat: 16 g, Saturated fat: 5.3 g, Carbohydrate: 33 g, Protein: 21 g, Sugar: 12 g, Sodium: 520 mg, Dietary fibre: 3 g, Cholesterol: 55 mg

Ginger Lemon Sticky Chicken

PREP TIME: 5 MIN. **COOK TIME:** 20 MIN.
SERVES: 4 servings

INGREDIENTS:
- 2 tablespoon lemon juice
- 3 tablespoon filtered water
- 3 tablespoon honey
- 1 teaspoon Red Boat fish sauce
- 2 teaspoon fresh grated ginger
- 2 crushed garlic cloves
- 1-2 tablespoon oil
- 4 chicken thighs, skin on, boneless
- 1 teaspoon arrowroot powder
- 1 tablespoon filtered water
- ¼ chopped green onion

COOKING INSTRUCTIONS:
1. Mix together vigorously the lemon juice, water, honey, fish sauce, ginger and garlic together in a small bowl and set aside.
2. Heat oil over medium heat in a large skillet. Add chicken thighs skin-side down. Allow to cook for about 3-5 minutes.
3. Turn heat to medium and allow the thighs to cook for about 5-7 more minutes.
4. Flip the thighs and allow to cook for about 4 minutes on the other side.
5. Add the lemon-ginger mixture. Reduce the heat and simmer for some minutes.

6. Stir together the arrowroot powder and water. Add to the skillet and stir for 2 minutes. Then remove from heat.
7. Serve thigh and garnish with freshly chopped green onion.

NUTRITIONAL INFO:
Calories: 782, Total fat: 45.7 g, Saturated fat: 6.5 g, Carbohydrate: 2.1 g, Protein: 65 g, Sodium: 461.7 mg, Vitamin C: 15 mg, Dietary fibre: 4.8 g, Cholesterol: 92.3 mg

Creamy Leek and Salmon Soup

PREP TIME: 5 MIN. **COOK TIME:** 30 MIN.
SERVES: 5 servings

INGREDIENTS:
- 2 tablespoon avocado oil
- 3 minced cloves garlic
- 4 leeks washed and sliced
- 1/3 coconut milk
- Chicken broth
- 1 lb. salmon
- Salt
- 2 tablespoon dried thyme leaves

COOKING INSTRUCTIONS:
1. Heat the avocado oil in a sauce pan at a low temperature
2. Add chopped leeks and garlics and cook for about 10-15 minutes
3. Pour the stock and thyme, then simmer for about another 10-15 minutes and add season

4. Add salt
5. Add the salmon and the coconut milk to the pan
6. Simmer gently and cook until the fish is tender
7. Serve warm

NUTRITIONAL INFO:
Calories: 668, Total fat: 23 g, Saturated fat:5.6g, Carbohydrate: 27.9 g, Protein: 4.1 g, Sugar: 3.7 g, Sodium: 915.3 mg, Potassium: 622.9 mg, Dietary fibre: 3.4 g, Cholesterol: 13.0 g

Onion Soup

PREP TIME: 5 MIN. **COOK TIME:** 15 MIN.
SERVES: 4 servings

INGREDIENTS:
- 2 tablespoon avocado oil
- 6 cups of pork stock
- 2 sprigs of fresh thyme
- 2 bay leaves
- 1kg yellow onions
- 1 tablespoon salt
- 1 tablespoon balsamic vinegar

COOKING INSTRUCTIONS:
1. Set instant pot to sauté and add oil
2. Cut the onions and slice
3. Cook the onions until they have become translucent
4. Add the balsamic vinegar and scrape up any fond from the bottom of the instant pot
5. Add the stock, salt, bay leaves and thyme
6. Turn off the instant pot and make sure to check that the float is free and vent isn't blocked
7. Set instant pot to high pressure and cook the soup for about 8-10 minutes

8. Discard the bay leaves and thyme stems, then blend the soup together by transferring the soup carefully to a blender
9. Serve warm

NUTRITIONAL INFO:
Calories: 341, Total fat: 0.7 g, Saturated fat: 0.05 g, Carbohydrate: 3.3 g, Protein: 1.5 g, Sugar: 1.3 g, Sodium: 423 mg, Dietary fibre: 0.3 g, Cholesterol: 0.02 mg

Pomegranate Chicken Salad

PREP TIME: 10 MINUTES, **COOK TIME:** 0 MINUTE
SERVES: 2 servings

INGREDIENTS:
- 1 sliced avocado
- 2 orange segments
- 1 tablespoon sea salt
- ¼ cup pomegranate seeds
- 1 cup shredded chicken
- Extra virgin olive oil
- ½ lb. spinach

COOKING INSTRUCTIONS:
1. Mix the juice from the 2 orange segments together with 3 tablespoon of virgin oil
2. Toss the dressing with spinach, sea salt and chicken
3. Sprinkle on the pomegranate seeds on the surface
4. Add the avocado on the surface as well
5. Now you are ready

NUTRITIONAL INFO:
Calories: 470, Total fat: 37 g, Saturated fat: 13.7 g, Carbohydrate: 16 g, Protein: 24 g, Sugar: 3 g, Sodium: 374 mg, Dietary fibre: 10 g, Cholesterol: 87 mg

Baked Chicken Thighs

PREP TIME: 5 MINUTES, **COOK TIME:** 35 MINUTES
SERVES: 2 servings

INGREDIENTS:
- 4 chicken thighs
- 2 tablespoon balsamic vinegar
- I inch cube ginger
- 1 cup daikon radish
- ¼ cup olive oil
- 2 zucchinis
- ½ cup sliced carrot

COOKING INSTRUCTIONS:
1. Preheat oven to about 350° Fahrenheit. Debone chicken thigh and dry with paper tower
2. Wrap the skins around the thighs and arrange on a greased baking sheet
3. Slice veggies and arrange them around the chicken
4. Mix together vigorously sauce ingredient and pour over chicken and veggies
5. Season with salt and pepper
6. Bake for about 25-30 minutes
7. Broil for about 3-5 minutes for extra crispiness

NUTRITIONAL INFO:
Calories: 346, Total fat: 15.3 g, Saturated fat: 6.1 g, Carbohydrate: 3.7 g, Protein: 29.6 g, Sodium: 99 mg, Potassium: 256 mg, Dietary fibre: 2.3 g, Cholesterol: 105 mg

Beef Lettuce Wraps

PREP TIME: 10 MINUTES, **COOK TIME:** 20 MINUTES
SERVES: 4-6 servings

INGREDIENTS:
- 2 lbs. lean ground beef
- 3 cloves crushed garlic
- 3 tablespoon fish sauce
- 2/3 cups of very finely chopped mint
- 2/3 cups of very finely chopped cilantro
- Head romaine lettuce
- 1/3 cup of fresh lemon juice
- 2 cups beef broth

COOKING INSTRUCTIONS:
1. Brown the beef in a large skillet over medium-high heat, breaking up frequently with a spoon for about 8-10
2. Add broth to beef. Let simmer and stir occasionally and broth has completely boiled away
3. Once there's no water, stir in the lemon juice mixture. Simmer until the lemon has just boiled away
4. Stir in chopped herbs and remove the beef from heat
5. Serve and enjoy

NUTRITIONAL INFO:
Calories: 216, Total fat: 8.7 g, Saturated fat: 2.8 g, Carbohydrate: 10.3 g, Protein: 24.7 g, Sodium: 1094.3 mg, Potassium:679.5 mg, Dietary fibre: 3.1 g, Cholesterol: 56.7 mg

Steak Salad with Arugula

PREP TIME: 5 MINUTES, **COOK TIME:** 20 MINUTES
SERVES: 4 servings

INGREDIENTS:
- 1 lemon
- 12 oz. steak
- 5 oz. baby arugula
- Black pepper, to taste
- Extra virgin olive oil
- Sea salt, to taste

COOKING INSTRUCTIONS:
1. Preheat oven to about 375°F. Sprinkle both sides of the steak(s) with salt and pepper.
2. Heat large oven-proof skillet over medium-high heat for 5 minutes. Add steaks to dry pan and sear for 2 minutes a side.
3. Put the skillet in the preheated oven and cook for about 6 minutes, until it reaches an internal temperature of 135 degrees.
4. When the steak is done, set it in a warm place to rest for 5-10 minutes. His allow the juice to settle into the meat, rather than on your cutting board when you slice it.
5. While the steak rests, place arugula in a large bowl, drizzle with olive oil and the juice of ½ lemon. Sprinkle liberally with salt and toss to blend. Taste and add more oil, lemon juice or salt as needed. Divide between two plates.
6. Slice the steaks into bite-size pieces, diagonally across the grain. Scatter the steak pieces on top of the plates with the arugula.
7. Lastly, pour steak juices from the cutting board on top, and sprinkle one more time with a little pepper.
8. Serve and savor every bite!

NUTRITIONAL INFO:
Calories: 304, Total fat: 72 g, Saturated fat: 18 g, Carbohydrate: 27.6 g, Protein: 34.5 g, Sodium: 537.5 mg, Dietary fibre: 0.9 g, Cholesterol: 49.0 mg

Broccoli Beef

PREP TIME: 5 MINUTES, **COOK TIME:** 15 MINUTES
SERVES: 2 servings

INGREDIENTS:
- 2 cups of broccoli florets
- ½ lb. beef, sliced thin and precooked
- 3 cloves garlic, crushed or use garlic powder
- 1 teaspoon freshly grated ginger or use ginger powder
- 2 tablespoons of coconut aminos or tamari sauce to taste
- Coconut oil to cook in

COOKING INSTRUCTIONS:
1. Place two tablespoons of coconut oil into a skillet or saucepan on medium heat. Add the broccoli florets into the skillet.
2. When the broccoli softens to the amount you want, add in the beef.
3. Saute for 2 minutes and then add in the garlic, ginger, and coconut aminos/tamari sauce.
4. Serve and enjoy.

NUTRITIONAL INFO:
Calories: 150, Total fat: 7 g, Saturated fat: 2 g, Carbohydrate: 13 g, Protein: 9 g, Sugar: 7 g, Sodium: 520 mg, Dietary fibre: 2 g, Cholesterol: 12 mg

AIP Snacks and Desserts Recipes

Done with your meal? Sneak in a dessert! Can't have a meal? Have a snack. Here are 15 different snacks and desserts recipes for your enjoyment!

SNACKS

Zucchini Fries

PREP TIME: 5 MINUTES, **COOK TIME:** 55 MINUTES
SERVES: 4 servings

INGREDIENTS:
- 2-3 large zucchini
- 3 oz. package of pork rinds
- ¼ cup of olive oil

COOKING INSTRUCTIONS:
1. Preheat oven to 400°F and line 2 baking trays with parchment paper
2. Cut zucchini into fry shape pieces
3. Finely grind pork rinds in a food processor and pour into a baking dish
4. Place zucchini and olive oil in a large zip top bag and shake to coat with oil
5. Remove zucchini pieces from bag, a few pieces at a time dredge with pork rinds and place on baking trays in a single layer without them touching
6. Bake for about 30 minutes at 400°F until golden brown and crisp
7. Flip over after 25 minutes

NUTRITIONAL INFO:
Calories: 172, Total fat: 8.58 g, Saturated fat: 3.6 g, Carbohydrate: 11.8 g, Protein: 13.9 g, Sugar:5.6 g, Sodium: 292 mg, Potassium: 866 mg, Cholesterol: 20 mg, Dietary fibre: 3.6 g

Tigernut Cheese Cracker

PREP TIME: 10 MINUTES, **COOK TIME:** 20 MINUTES
SERVES: 2 servings

INGREDIENTS:
- 1 cup of tigernut flour
- 1 tablespoon gelatine
- ½ teaspoon turmeric powder
- 1 teaspoon sea salt
- ¼ cup of water
- 1 tablespoon nutritional yeast
- 3 tablespoons coconut oil
- ½ teaspoon black pepper (can be omitted)

COOKING INSTRUCTIONS:
1. Preheat the oven to 350°F. In a medium mixing bowl, combine the tigernut flour, coconut oil, nutritional yeast, turmeric and salt. Set the mixture aside.
2. Pour ¼ cup of water into a small sauce pan and add to a stove top. Slowly sprinkle the gelatine into the water and allow it to bloom for 1-2 minutes. Turn the heat on for 2-3 minutes to allow the gelatine to melt. Remove the pot from the heat and quickly mix together vigorously until it foams.
3. Pour the gelatine egg into the dough and stir quickly to combine.
4. Line a baking sheet with parchment paper and place the dough onto the paper. Place another sheet of parchment paper on top of the dough, sandwiching it between two pieces of parchment paper.

5. Flatten the dough through the top piece of parchment paper until it's thin and even.
6. Using a knife, slice the dough into crackers.
7. Bake the crackers for 8-12 minutes or until crisped to liking. Remove from the oven and allow to cool before using a spatula to remove from the pan.
8. Serve immediately or store in the fridge.

NUTRITIONAL INFO:
Calories: 35, Total fat: 2.2 g, Saturated fat: 0.3 g, Carbohydrate: 2.8 g, Protein: 0.5 g, Sodium: 378 mg, Dietary fibre: 0.8 g, Cholesterol: 35 mg

Asian Stuffed Mushrooms

PREP TIME: 15 MINUTES, **COOK TIME:** 15 MINUTES
SERVES: 4 servings

INGREDIENTS:
- 20 medium white button mushrooms
- ½ lb. (225 g)
- 2 finely chopped green onions
- 6 cloves of garlic, minced
- 1 tablespoon minced ginger
- 1 teaspoon salt
- 4 tablespoons of coconut aminos
- ½ teaspoon apple cider vinegar

COOKING INSTRUCTIONS:
1. Combine the ground chicken, green onions, ginger, garlic, coconut aminos, and salt in a mixing bowl and mix well
2. Clean the mushrooms. Using your hands stuff the meat mixture into the mushrooms.
3. You can either bake or steam these.
4. Mix the garlic, coconut aminos, and vinegar in a small bowl together to make the dipping sauce.
5. Serve the steamed stuffed mushrooms with the dipping sauce.

NUTRITIONAL INFO:

Calories: 105, Total fat: 2 g, Saturated fat: 0.7 g, Carbohydrate: 12 g, Protein: 13 g, Sugar: 6 g, Dietary fibre: 4 g, Cholesterol: 0.9 mg

Salmon Cakes

PREP TIME: 10 MINUTES, **COOK TIME:** 30 MINUTES
SERVES: 2 servings

INGREDIENTS:
- 10 oz. salmon (270g), (canned or cooked filets and flaked)
- 1 tablespoon of fresh dill (6 g), finely chopped
- 28 g cup of coconut flour
- 32 g of arrowroot flour
- ¼ cup of coconut oil
- Salt to taste

COOKING INSTRUCTIONS:
1. Preheat oven to 350°F.
2. Mix all the ingredients together in a mixing bowl.
3. Line a baking tray with parchment paper.
4. Form the mixture into small flat cakes.
5. Place on the lined baking tray and bake for 25-30 minutes.
6. Remove the tray from the oven and let the salmon cakes cool before removing.
7. Enjoy with some coconut cream and a light salad.

NUTRITIONAL INFO:
Calories: 560, Total fat: 39 g, Saturated fat: 12.1 g, Carbohydrate: 20 g, Protein: 41 g, Sugar: 1 g Dietary fibre: 5 g, Cholesterol: 12 mg

Pumpkin Granola

PREP TIME: 5 MINUTES, **COOK TIME:** 15 MINUTES
SERVES: 3 servings

INGREDIENTS:
- 1 tablespoon pumpkin puree
- 2 tablespoon coconut oil, melted
- 1 tablespoon maple syrup
- 2 teaspoon cinnamon
- Sub mace
- ½ teaspoon sea salt

COOKING INSTRUCTIONS:
1. Preheat the oven to 350°F and line a baking sheet with parchment paper
2. Pour all of the dry ingredients into a large bowl and mix
3. Add in the pumpkin puree, maple syrup, coconut oil and stir to evenly coat
4. Spoon the mixture out onto the baking sheet and bake for about 10-12 minutes
5. Keep a close eye on the granola to ensure it doesn't burn
6. Remove from the oven and allow to cool
7. Store in the fridge for 5-7 days and serve over paleo pancakes, coconut yogurt or as a snack itself

NUTRITIONAL INFO:
Calories: 160, Total fat: 10 g, Saturated fat: 3.4 g, Carbohydrate: 2.1 g, Protein: 6 g, Sugar: 10 g, Sodium: 325 mg, Dietary fibre: 5 g, Cholesterol: 8g

DESSERT

Maple-Cinnamon Sweet Potatoes

PREP TIME: 5 MIN. **SERVES:** 4 servings
INGREDIENTS:
- 4 small sweet potatoes
- ¾ teaspoon cinnamon
- ¼ cup of maple syrup

COOKING INSTRUCTIONS:
1. Preheat oven to 400°F.
2. Pierce the sweet potatoes with a fork severally.
3. Place the sweet potatoes on baking sheet lined with foil and bake for about 45-60 minutes.
4. Mix the syrup and cinnamon together.
5. Serve on top of the baked potatoes.

NUTRITIONAL INFO:

Calories: 270, Total fat: 2 g, Saturated fat: 0.8 g, Carbohydrate: 34 g, Protein: 2.1 g, Sugar: 7 g, Dietary fibre: 4.7 g, Cholesterol: 0.3 mg

Raw Strawberry Papaya Ice Cream Tart

PREP TIME: 15 MINUTES
SEERVES: 7" tart

INGREDIENTS:
- 2 cups of frozen papaya chunks
- 2 cups of dried white mulberries
- 1 cup of frozen strawberries
- 2-4 tablespoon maple syrup
- A small handful of basil
- 10-12 soft pitted medjool dates

COOKING INSTRUCTIONS:
1. Place all crust ingredients into a food processor and process into a sticky crumble.
2. Transfer into a tart pan and press into shape to form a shell.
3. Place into the freezer to firm up.
4. Place all filling ingredients into a clean food processor and process until smooth.
5. Scoop this mixture into the prepared tart crust and smooth out the top and place back into the freezer for at least 55-60 minutes to firm up fully.
6. Keep frozen and enjoy slices as needed.

NUTRITIONAL INFO:
Calories: 93, Total fat: 0.9 g, Saturated fat: 0.03 g, Carbohydrate: 27.4 g, Protein: 2.3 g, Sugar: 17 g, Calcium: 18 mg, Dietary fibre: 2.1 g, Cholesterol: 22 mg, Vitamin C: 46 mg

2-Ingredients Banana Fudge

PREP TIME: 25 MINUTES
SERVES: 4 servings

INGREDIENTS:
- 6 ripe bananas
- Ground cardamom
- Crushed nuts for garnish
- 3 tablespoons coconut oil, divided

COOKING INSTRUCTIONS:
1. Put the bananas in a blender and puree.
2. Melt 1 tablespoon of coconut oil in a non-stick sauté pan over medium heat and then add the banana puree.
3. Stir continuously for about 15-20 minutes.
4. Add 1 tablespoon of coconut oil and stir rigorously, then add the final tablespoon of coconut oil and continue to stir until the banana mixture turns dark and sticky.
5. Spoon the banana mixture onto a greased plate or in a parchment-lined loaf pan and allow it to cool in the fridge.
6. Cut the fudge when cold, and then allow it to come to room temperature before serving.

NUTRITIONAL INFO:
Calories: 607, Total fat: 6 g, Saturated fat: 1.8 g, Carbohydrate: 87.6 g, Protein: 7.9 g, Sugar: 19 g, Calcium: 36.7 mg, Dietary fibre: 7.9 g, Cholesterol: 16 mg

Coconut Plantain Macaroons

PREP TIME: 15 MIN. **COOK TIME:** 30 MIN.
SERVES: 9 servings

INGREDIENTS:
- 1 yellow plantain
- 1 tablespoon virgin coconut oil
- 1¼ cup of organic coconut chips
- 3 teaspoon ceylon cinnamon
- ¼ cup of organic maple syrup

COOKING INSTRUCTIONS:
1. Preheat oven to 375°F.
2. Combine peeled plantain, coconut oil, cinnamon, and maple syrup and puree completely in a food processor.
3. Combine pureed plantain mixture and shredded coconut in a large mixing bowl and mash the ingredients together with a fork.
4. Scoop out 3-4 tablespoons of the mixture and form a round macaroon. An ice cream scoop might be used depending on your choice.
5. Bake until macaroons begin to brown around edges.
6. Serve and enjoy.

NUTRITIONAL INFO:
Calories: 136, Total fat: 0.9 g, Saturated fat: 0.02 g, Carbohydrate: 40.6 g, Protein: 2.6 g, Iron: 0.9 mg, Calcium: 2.6 mg, Dietary fibre: 2.6 mg, Cholesterol: 31 mg

Chewy Cinnamon Sugar Cookies

PREP TIME: 10 MINUTE, **COOK TIME:** 20 MINUTES
SERVES: 3 servings

INGREDIENTS:
- 1 yellow-green plantain
- 3 tablespoon room temperature non-hydrogenated palm shortening
- Pinch of salt
- ¾ teaspoon cinnamon
- ¼ cup of maple sugar
- ¼ cup of water chestnut flour
- ¼ teaspoon baking soda

COOKING INSTRUCTIONS:
1. Preheat oven to 350°F and line a baking sheet with parchment paper.
2. Peel, chop, and place plantain in a food container fitted with the "S" blade.
3. Allow machine to run until plantain begins to break down into a smooth paste.
4. Add baking soda, water, chestnut flour, palm shortening, cinnamon, pinch of salt, baking soda, and granulated sweetener (any of choice) letting food processor run until everything is fully incorporated.
5. Using a cookie scoop, dollop cookie dough onto lined baking sheet, flatten with the back of your scoop and bake for about 15-20 minutes.
6. Remove from oven and serve cold.

NUTRITIONAL INFO:
Calories: 176, Total fat: 4.6 g, Saturated fat: 1.9 g, Carbohydrate: 36.8 g, Protein: 12 g   Calcium: 2.8 mg, Iron: 0.6 mg, Dietary fibre: 3.7 g, Cholesterol: 42 mg

AIP Drinks Recipes

Now we cap off our amazing list of recipes with the AIP drinks recipes, enjoy!

Stone Fruit Smoothie

PREP TIME: 5 MIN. **COOK TIME:** 2 MIN.
SERVES: 2 servings

INGREDIENTS:

- 1 small pitted and sliced apricot
- 1 cup full-fat coconut milk
- 1 tablespoon collagen powder
- 4-7 ice cubes
- 1 small pitted and sliced plum
- ½ cup cooled strong black tea

COOKING INSTRUCTIONS:
1. Place all ingredients in a blender.
2. Blend until smooth.

NUTRITIONAL INFO:
Calories: 164, Total fat: 5.2 g, Saturated fat: 2.3 g, Carbohydrate: 36.6 g, Protein: 2 g, Sugar: 12 g, Dietary fibre: 4.1 g, Cholesterol: 42 mg

AIP Margarita Mocktail

PREP TIME: 13 MINUTES
SERVES: 4 servings

INGREDIENTS:
- 1 cup of filtered water
- 1 cup of coconut palm sugar
- ½ cup of lemon juice (about 3 lemons juiced)
- ½ cup of orange juice (about 1 orange juiced)
- 1 cup of citrus-flavored kombucha
- 1 cup of lemon-flavored sparkling water (like La Croix)
- 40 ice cubes
- Course sea salt
- Lemon slices to garnish

INSTRUCTIONS:
1. Mix water, sugar, lemon, and orange juice in a sauce pan. Bring to a boil and stir to completely dissolve sugar (should result in just over 2 cups of simple syrup).
2. Place syrup mixture in refrigerator to cool completely.
3. Mix kombucha and sparkling water together. Add 1 cup completely cooled syrup (the rest can be stored in a sealed jar in the refrigerator) and stir.
4. Add mix with ice cubes to blender, adding more ice as you blend, until almost the consistency of a "slushy."
5. Use lemon garnish to wet rim of drinking glasses, turn upside down in salt to salt rim. Fill glasses and enjoy!

NUTRITIONAL INFO:
Calories: 224, Total fat: 0.8 g, Saturated fat: 0.2 g, Carbohydrate: 32 g, Protein: 1.8 g Sugar: 21 g, Sodium: 324 mg, Dietary fibre: 3.9 g, Vitamin C: 39 mg, Cholesterol: 32 mg

Strawberry-Hibiscus Iced Tea

PREP TIME: 1 HOUR
SERVES: 16 servings

INGREDIENTS:
- 8 cups water
- 1½ tablespoon dried mint
- 1½ tablespoon dried hibiscus flowers
- 1 lb. strawberries, hulled
- ¼ cup lemon juice
- 2 tablespoon honey
- Ice, to serve

INSTRUCTIONS:
1. Bring the water to a boil and combine the mint and hibiscus in a tea ball.
2. In a large pitcher or tea pot, pour the water over the tea ball and steep for 15 minutes.
3. Remove the tea ball and discard its contents. Allow the tea to cool to room temperature, then chill in the fridge for at least 30 minutes.
4. Transfer 1 cup of the tea to a blender and add the strawberries, lemon juice, and honey. Puree until smooth, then stir back into the tea.
5. Serve over ice.

NUTRITIONAL INFO:
Calories: 268, Total fat: 1 g, Saturated fat: 0.2 g, Carbohydrate: 8 g, Protein: 2.5 g, Sugar: 12 g, Vitamin C: 86 mg, Dietary fibre: 4.3 g, Cholesterol: 2.4 mg

Watermelon-Basil Shrub

PREP TIME: 10 MINUTES
SERVES: 15 servings

INGREDIENTS:
- ½ medium watermelon, cubed, rind removed (approx. 5-6 cups)
- 1 large bunch basil, chopped
- ½ cup honey
- ½ cup white balsamic vinegar
- Sparkling mineral water
- Ice

INSTRUCTIONS:
1. Crush and mix melon, basil, and honey in large, glass bowl or jar. Cover tightly and allow to macerate in refrigerator for 2-3 days.
2. Pour fruit mixture into blender and process until smooth.
3. Strain through cheesecloth to remove seeds and pulp. (You should have approx. 2½-3 cups juice.)
4. Mix juice with vinegar.
5. Pour ¼-1/2 cup each in bottom of serving glasses, depending on the flavor strength you like.
6. Fill glass with ice and add sparkling water to fill.
7. Serve and enjoy!

NUTRITIONAL INFO:
Calories: 322, Total fat: 0.9 g, Saturated fat: 0.5 g, Carbohydrate: 42 g, Protein: 2.3 g, Sugar: 15 g, Dietary fibre: 2.4 g, Cholesterol: 64 mg

Strawberry Ginger swizzle

PREP TIME: 10 MINUTES
SERVES: 16 servings

INGREDIENTS:
- ¼ cup raw organic unfiltered apple cider vinegar
- 1 organic lemon juice
- 1 inch piece of fresh ginger root, peeled and thinly sliced
- 8 cups filtered water
- 1/3 cup raw honey
- 1 cup sliced organic strawberries

INSTRUCTIONS:
1. Add all ingredients to a large mason jar.
2. Cover with lid and shake to combine.
3. Place in the refrigerator for up to 24 hours.
4. Strain and serve cold.

NUTRITIONAL INFO:
Calories: 286, Total fat: 1.2 g, Saturated fat: 0.4 g, Carbohydrate: 45 g, Protein: 3.5 g, Vitamin C: 186 mg, Dietary fibre: 3.9 g, Cholesterol: 3.5 mg

AIP Coffee

PREP TIME: 5 MINUTES, **COOK TIME**: 8 MINUTES
SERVES: 3 servings

INGREDIENTS:
- 1 tablespoon roasted dandelion root
- 3 cups water
- 1 tablespoon carob powder
- 1 pitted date
- 1 tablespoon roasted chicory powder

INSTRUCTIONS:
1. Combine all ingredients in a small saucepan and boil.
2. Lower the heat and allow the mixture to simmer for about 5-7 minutes.
3. Remove from heat.
4. Strain and serve.

NUTRITIONAL INFO:
Calories: 164, Total fat: 2.8 g, Saturated fat: 0.8 g, Carbohydrate: 15.3 g, Protein: 2.5 g, Sugar: 12.6 g, Dietary fibre: 0.9 g, Cholesterol: 2.6 mg

Berry Fizz Mocktail

PREP TIME: 10 MINUTES
SERVES: 1 serving

INGREDIENTS:
- 8 raspberries
- 75 ml pomegranate juice
- Fresh lemon juice
- Sparkling water
- 90 ml tart cherry juice

INSTRUCTIONS:
1. Add the raspberries and lemon juice to a pint sized mason jar and use a cocktail muddler to gently press the raspberries into the lemon juice.
2. Add the tart cherry and pomegranate juices to the jar.
3. Put the lid on the jar and add a few ice cubes then shake to combine. Remove the lid then top the drink off with sparkling water.
4. Garnish with a few extra raspberries and a lemon slice then serve.

NUTRITIONAL INFO:
Calories: 196, Total fat: 0.9 g, Saturated fat: 0.02 g, Carbohydrate: 23.8 g, Protein: 3.6 g, Sugar: 17.6 g, Dietary fibre: 4.2 g, Cholesterol: 5.9 mg

Paleo Cardio Green Juice

PREP TIME: 10 MINUTES
SERVES: 1 serving

INGREDIENTS:
- 6 cups Kale
- 1 cup Blueberries
- 2 cups cucumber
- 2 cups fresh Mint leaves
- 2 cups Granny Smith apples

INSTRUCTIONS:
1. Wash the kale, mint, and blueberries.
2. Scrub and wash the cucumber and apples. You don't need to peel them if they're organic because you need to keep the nutrients.
3. Add all ingredients to a juicer.
4. Serve and enjoy.

NUTRITIONAL INFO:
Calories: 256, Total fat: 1 g, Saturated fat: 0.2 g, Carbohydrate: 12.6 g, Protein: 7.3 g, Sugar : 1 g, Dietary fibre: 2.6 g, Cholesterol: 2.5 mg

Pineapple Smoothie

PREP TIME: 10 MINUTES
SERVES: 2 servings

INGREDIENTS:
- 3 cups fresh Pineapple
- ½ teaspoon raw Honey
- 1 cup Coconut Milk
- ¼ teaspoon Vanilla Extract
- 1 cup Coconut Water

INSTRUCTIONS:
1. Blend the pineapple, coconut milk, coconut water, honey and vanilla together until smooth.
2. Add 8 ice cubes to your blender for thicker, icier smoothie.

NUTRITIONAL INFO:
Calories: 106, Total fat: 2.5 g, Saturated fat: 0.7 g, Carbohydrate: 22.5 g, Protein: 4.8 g, Dietary fibre: 2.5 g, Cholesterol: 2.5 mg

Watermelon Aqua Fresca

PREP TIME: 10 MINUTES
SERVES: 9 cups

INGREDIENTS:
- 9 cups seedless watermelon chunks
- 3 inch piece of fresh ginger
- Sea salt, coarse
- 6-8 sprigs of fresh mint
- Lemon slices
- Fresh mint
- 5-6 lemons juice
- Sparkling water

INSTRUCTIONS:
1. Fill blender with watermelon chunks about 3/4 full beneath the max fill line. Add the ginger, lemon juice and fresh mint.
2. Blend until watermelon juice has no visible bits.
3. Place a fine mesh strainer over a large pitcher and pour the watermelon juice through to strain out the pulp a little at a time.
4. Use a spoon to stir up and press down on the pulp each time, then remove and discard it. Continue this process until all of the juice has been strained. Add the remaining watermelon to the blender and juice it.
5. Refrigerate and serve chill.

NUTRITIONAL INFO:
Calories: 32, Total fat: 0.6 g, Saturated fat: 0.02 g, Carbohydrate: 8.6 g, Protein: 1.6 g
Sodium: 234.2 mg, Vitamin C: 57.4 mg, Dietary fibre: 0.3 g, Cholesterol: 1.3 mg

Chapter 3
A 14-day meal plan

Now we have a whole bunch of recipes on our plates, let's work on creating a simple 14-day meal plan for you to begin your AIP with.

Week 1

DAY	BREAKFAST	LUNCH	DINNER	SNACK AND DESSERT
SUNDAY	Apple-Sage Pork Skillet	Calamari Summer Salad	Shrimp Scampi	Zucchini Fries
MONDAY	Fries with Bacon Chive Crumble	Shrimp Salad with Gillantro Lemon Ranch Dressing	Pumpkin Chili	Tigernut Cheese Cracker
TUESDAY	Turkey Sausage	Orange-glazed Pork Tenderloin	Creamy Garlic Spaghetti Squash Casserole	Mapple-Cinnamon Sweet Potatoes
WEDNESDAY	Rissoto With Greens	Zuppa Toscana	Italian Calzone	Raw Strawberry Papaya Ice Cream Tart

THURSDAY	Apple-Sage Skillet	Strawberry-Hibiscus Iced Tea	Hearty Salmon Crowder	Pumpkin Granola
FRIDAY	Squash Browns	Honey-Lemon Glazed Salmon	Creaky Leek and Salmon Soup	2-Ingredients Bananas Fudge
SATURDAY	Porridge with Lemon And Berries	Crispy Drill Fried Fish	Beef Lettuce Wraps	Coconut Plantain macaroons

Week 2

DAY	BREAKFAST	LUNCH	DINNER	SNACK AND DESSERT
SUNDAY	Moroccan Inspired Skillet	Carrot, Cucumber And Avocado Salad	Onion Soup	Asian Stuffed Mushrooms
MONDAY	Stone Fruit Smoothie	Grilled Chicken Thigh with Pineapple Mint Salsa	Stack Salad with Arugula	Salmon Cakes
TUESDAY	Italian-Spiced 50/50 Sausages	Watermelon - Basil Shrub	Broccoli Beef	Chewy Cinnamon Sugar Cookies

WEDNESDAY	Fries with Bacon Chive Crumble	Wild Salmon with Zucchini Noodles, Baby Leaves and A Basil Dressing	Pomegranate Chicken Salad	Pumpkin Granola
THURSDAY	Turkey Sausage	Zuppa Toscana	Mini Lasagna	Raw Strawberry Papaya Ice Cream Tart
FRIDAY	Porridge with Lemon and Berries	Calamari Summer Salad	Chicken Salsa Verde Tacos with Lemon	Tigernut Cheese Cracker
SATURDAY	Squash Browns	Orange-glazed Pork Tenderloin	Ginger-Lemon Sticky Chicken	2-Ingredients Bananas Fudge

The purpose of creating a meal plan is to go ahead and prepare them beforehand. Create a check list of ingredients you have, shop for the ones you don't and prepare the meals and have them ready to go.

Made in the USA
San Bernardino, CA
09 December 2018